Yummy Toddler Food

Copyright-All Rights Reserved

This book has copyright protection.You can use the book for personal purpose.You should not see,use,alter,distribute,quote,take excerpts or paraphrase in part or whole the material contained in this book without obtaining the permission of the author first.

Introduction

"Yummy Toddler Food" is a delightful and practical cookbook designed specifically to make mealtime a joyous adventure for your little ones. Created with love and expertise, this cookbook is packed with a wide array of nutritious and delicious recipes that will delight the taste buds of even the pickiest eaters.

Featuring over 70 creative and easy-to-follow recipes, "Yummy Toddler Food" is a treasure trove of ideas to help parents and caregivers provide wholesome meals that toddlers will eagerly devour. From finger foods and snacks to main courses and desserts, each recipe has been thoughtfully crafted to cater to the unique nutritional needs of growing children while introducing them to a variety of flavors and textures.

Inside this cookbook, you'll find a collection of mouthwatering recipes that are both appealing to the eye and packed with essential nutrients. Discover clever ways to sneak in vegetables, fruits, whole grains, and lean proteins, ensuring your toddler receives a balanced and nourishing diet.

The recipes in "Yummy Toddler Food" are not only healthy but also designed to inspire creativity and encourage family participation in the kitchen. With helpful tips on ingredient substitutions, food allergies, and toddler-friendly cooking techniques, this cookbook becomes an invaluable resource for parents navigating the sometimes-challenging world of feeding toddlers.

Whether you're a seasoned chef or a novice in the kitchen, "Yummy Toddler Food" empowers you to create tasty, nutritious, and visually appealing meals that your little ones will love. From vibrant smoothies and colorful veggie muffins to adorable mini pizzas and homemade chicken nuggets, this cookbook turns mealtime into an enjoyable bonding experience that sets the foundation for a lifetime of healthy eating habits.

With "Yummy Toddler Food" as your guide, you can embark on a culinary journey that fosters your toddler's adventurous palate and makes every meal a celebration of taste and nutrition. Get ready to witness your little ones' eyes light up with joy as they discover the wonders of delicious and wholesome food!

The Best Buttermilk Pancakes

Ingredients:

1 cup all-purpose flour
1 tablespoon sugar
1 teaspoon baking powder
1/2 teaspoon baking soda
1/4 teaspoon salt
1 cup buttermilk (or substitute with 1 cup milk mixed with 1 tablespoon vinegar or lemon juice and let it sit for 5 minutes)
1 large egg
2 tablespoons unsalted butter, melted
Cooking spray or additional butter for greasing the pan

Instructions:

In a large bowl, whisk together the flour, sugar, baking powder, baking soda, and salt.
In a separate bowl, whisk together the buttermilk, egg, and melted butter until well combined.
Pour the wet ingredients into the dry ingredients and stir until just combined. Be careful not to overmix; a few lumps are fine.
Heat a non-stick skillet or griddle over medium heat. Lightly grease the surface with cooking spray or butter.
Pour about 1/4 cup of the pancake batter onto the skillet for each pancake.
Cook for 2-3 minutes until bubbles form on the surface of the pancake. Flip the pancake and cook for an additional 1-2 minutes until golden brown.
Remove the pancake from the skillet and let it cool slightly.
Repeat the process with the remaining batter until all the pancakes are cooked.
Allow the pancakes to cool further before serving to your baby.
These Buttermilk Pancakes are fluffy and delicious. They can be enjoyed by the whole family, including babies. Ensure that the pancakes are cooled adequately before serving to your baby. You can also adapt the recipe by cutting the pancakes into smaller pieces or mashing them for easier consumption, depending on your baby's age and eating abilities. Adjust the portion size based on your baby's age and appetite.

Vegetable Fritters

Ingredients:

1 cup grated vegetables (such as carrots, zucchini, or broccoli)
1/2 cup all-purpose flour
1/2 teaspoon baking powder
1/4 teaspoon salt
1/4 teaspoon garlic powder (optional)
1 egg, lightly beaten
2 tablespoons milk
2 tablespoons chopped fresh herbs (such as parsley or dill)
Olive oil or vegetable oil, for frying

Instructions:

In a large bowl, combine the grated vegetables. You can use a single vegetable or a mix of different ones according to your toddler's preference.
Squeeze out any excess moisture from the grated vegetables by pressing them between your hands or using a clean kitchen towel.
In a separate bowl, whisk together the flour, baking powder, salt, and garlic powder (if using).
Add the dry ingredients to the grated vegetables and stir to combine.
In a small bowl, whisk together the egg, milk, and chopped herbs. Pour the wet ingredients into the vegetable mixture and mix until well combined.
Heat a thin layer of oil in a large non-stick skillet over medium heat.
Scoop about 2 tablespoons of the fritter mixture and drop it into the skillet, pressing it down gently to form a flat fritter. Repeat with more mixture, leaving space between each fritter.
Cook the fritters for about 2-3 minutes on each side, or until golden brown and crispy. Adjust the heat if necessary to prevent burning.
Once cooked, transfer the fritters to a paper towel-lined plate to absorb any excess oil.
Allow the fritters to cool slightly before serving them to your toddler. They can be served warm or at room temperature.
Optional serving suggestions:
Serve the fritters with a side of plain yogurt or a homemade dipping sauce like a mild tomato sauce or tzatziki.
Include a side of sliced fruits or a small salad to round out the meal.
Remember to always supervise your toddler while eating and cut the fritters into small, toddler-sized pieces to avoid choking hazards. Enjoy!

Sugar Free Brownie

Ingredients

1 Egg.
1 Egg yolk.
1/2 Cup Avocado oil.
1/2 Cup Truvia *
1 tsp Vanilla.
1/3 Cup All purpose flour 48g.
1/3 Cup Cocoa powder 27g.
1/4 tsp Salt.

Sugar Free Brownies are a no-sugar dessert that can be enjoyed by those looking for healthier alternatives. This recipe uses no added sugar, yet still yields delicious and decadent brownies! To prepare this no-sugar dessert, start by preheating your oven to 350 degrees Fahrenheit. Then in a medium bowl, whisk together the egg and egg yolk. Next, pour in the avocado oil and Truvia, whisk until no lumps remain. Add in the vanilla extract and mix well. In a separate bowl, sift together the all-purpose flour, cocoa powder, and salt. Gradually add the dry ingredients to the wet ingredients and stir until no large clumps of flour remain. Grease an 8x8 baking pan with butter and pour in the batter. Bake for 25-30 minutes until a toothpick inserted into the center comes out clean. Allow the brownies to cool before serving, and enjoy this no-sugar dessert! With this recipe, you can indulge in delicious Sugar Free Brownies without the added sugar. Try this no-sugar dessert today and see for yourself how delicious no-sugar desserts can be!

Yoghurt Pancakes With Berries

Ingredients:

1/2 cup all-purpose flour
1/2 teaspoon baking powder
1/4 teaspoon baking soda
1/4 teaspoon ground cinnamon
1/2 cup plain Greek yogurt
1/4 cup milk (breast milk, formula, or regular milk)
1 tablespoon unsalted butter, melted
1 tablespoon maple syrup (optional)
1/4 cup mixed berries (such as blueberries, raspberries, or strawberries), chopped into small pieces
Cooking spray or additional butter for greasing the pan

Instructions:

In a bowl, whisk together the flour, baking powder, baking soda, and ground cinnamon.
In a separate bowl, combine the Greek yogurt, milk, melted butter, and maple syrup (if using). Mix until well combined.
Add the wet ingredients to the dry ingredients and stir until just combined. Be careful not to overmix; a few lumps are fine.
Gently fold in the chopped berries into the pancake batter.
Heat a non-stick skillet or griddle over medium heat. Lightly grease the surface with cooking spray or butter.
Pour about 1/4 cup of the pancake batter onto the skillet for each pancake.
Cook for 2-3 minutes until bubbles form on the surface of the pancake. Flip the pancake and cook for an additional 1-2 minutes until golden brown.
Remove the pancake from the skillet and let it cool slightly.
Repeat the process with the remaining batter until all the pancakes are cooked.
Allow the pancakes to cool further before serving to your baby.
These Yogurt Pancakes with Berries are a delicious and nutritious option for your baby's breakfast or snack. The addition of Greek yogurt provides a good source of protein and calcium, while the berries offer natural sweetness and antioxidants. Remember to cool the pancakes adequately before serving to your baby and adjust the portion size as needed based on their age and appetite.

Rainbow Fruit Cups with Greek Yogurt Dip

Ingredients:

Assorted fruits of various colors (such as strawberries, blueberries, kiwi, pineapple, grapes, and oranges)
1 cup Greek yogurt
1 tablespoon honey (optional, for sweetening the yogurt)

Instructions:

Wash and prepare the fruits. Remove any stems, pits, or seeds. Cut larger fruits like strawberries and kiwi into bite-sized pieces.
Arrange the fruits in separate bowls, grouping them by color to create a rainbow effect.
In a small bowl, combine the Greek yogurt and honey (if using) to make a sweet dip. Stir well to incorporate the honey into the yogurt.
Place the yogurt dip in a separate serving bowl.
Prepare small cups or bowls for serving the fruit. You can use clear plastic cups or any child-friendly containers.
To assemble the rainbow fruit cups, start by adding a layer of red fruits (e.g., strawberries or raspberries) at the bottom of each cup.
Continue adding fruits from each color group, layer by layer, creating a rainbow effect. For example, you can follow the order of red, orange, yellow, green, blue, and purple.
Leave a small space at the top of each cup for the yogurt dip.
Serve the rainbow fruit cups alongside the Greek yogurt dip.
Optional serving suggestions:
You can provide small skewers or toothpicks for your toddler to spear the fruits and dip them into the yogurt.
If your toddler prefers their fruit plain, you can skip the yogurt dip or serve it on the side for dipping.
This colorful and nutritious snack will surely be a hit with your toddler. Enjoy!

Mini Sweet Potato Muffins

Ingredients:

1 cup cooked and mashed sweet potato
1/2 cup unsweetened applesauce
1/4 cup maple syrup or honey
1/4 cup melted coconut oil or vegetable oil
2 eggs
1 teaspoon vanilla extract
1 cup whole wheat flour
1/2 cup all-purpose flour
1 teaspoon baking powder
1/2 teaspoon baking soda
1/2 teaspoon ground cinnamon
1/4 teaspoon salt

Instructions:

Preheat your oven to 350°F (175°C). Grease or line a mini muffin tin with paper liners.
In a large bowl, combine the mashed sweet potato, applesauce, maple syrup or honey, melted coconut oil or vegetable oil, eggs, and vanilla extract. Mix well until all the ingredients are combined.
In a separate bowl, whisk together the whole wheat flour, all-purpose flour, baking powder, baking soda, cinnamon, and salt.
Gradually add the dry ingredients to the wet ingredients, stirring until just combined. Be careful not to overmix, as it can make the muffins dense.
Spoon the batter into the prepared mini muffin tin, filling each cup about 2/3 full.
Bake for approximately 12-15 minutes or until a toothpick inserted into the center of a muffin comes out clean.
Remove the muffins from the oven and let them cool in the tin for a few minutes. Then transfer them to a wire rack to cool completely.
Optional variations:
You can add 1/4 cup of mini chocolate chips or chopped nuts (such as walnuts or pecans) to the batter for added texture and flavor.
You can also incorporate 1/2 cup of finely chopped fruits (such as apples or raisins) into the batter for extra sweetness and moisture.
These mini sweet potato muffins make a great on-the-go snack or a healthy addition to your toddler's lunchbox.
Enjoy!

Blueberry Muffins

Ingredients

1 ½ cups all-purpose flour. Great Value All-Purpose Flour, 5LB Bag.
¾ cup white sugar.
2 teaspoons baking powder.
½ teaspoon salt.
⅓ cup vegetable oil.
1 egg.
⅓ cup milk, or more as needed.
1 cup fresh blueberries.

Making a batch of delicious and healthy blueberry muffins is easy with the right ingredients. To begin, preheat your oven to 375°F (190°C). In a large bowl, combine 1 ½ cups all-purpose flour, ¾ cup white sugar, 2 teaspoons baking powder and ½ teaspoon salt. Add ⅓ cup vegetable oil and mix with a wooden spoon until the dry ingredients are moistened. Beat in 1 egg, then stir in ⅓ cup of milk. Gently fold in 1 cup fresh blueberries for a hint of sweetness and color.

Line your muffin tin with paper liners or spray it with cooking spray and fill each cup three-quarters full with the batter. Bake in preheated oven for 18 to 20 minutes, or until a toothpick inserted into the center of a muffin comes out clean. Let cool and enjoy your homemade blueberry muffins!

These healthy blueberry muffins are perfect as a snack or dessert, especially when baking with kids. They also make a great addition to a lunchbox and are sure to be a hit with the little ones! With this simple recipe, you can create tasty and nutritious treats in no time. So next time your family is looking for something sweet, whip up a batch of these blueberry muffins for an easy and healthy dessert. Enjoy!

Carrot Cake

Ingredients:

2 cups all-purpose flour
2 tsp baking powder
1 tsp baking soda
1 tsp cinnamon
1/2 tsp nutmeg
1/2 tsp salt
1/2 cup vegetable oil
1/2 cup unsweetened applesauce
1 cup granulated sugar
1/4 cup unsweetened almond milk
2 tsp vanilla extract
2 cups grated carrots
1/2 cup chopped walnuts (optional)
Vegan cream cheese frosting
(recipe below)

Instructions:

Preheat your oven to 350°F (180°C). Grease a 9-inch cake pan with cooking spray.
In a medium bowl, whisk together the flour, baking powder, baking soda, cinnamon, nutmeg, and salt until well combined.
In a large bowl, whisk together the vegetable oil, applesauce, sugar, almond milk, and vanilla extract until smooth.
Add the dry ingredients to the wet ingredients, stirring until just combined.
Fold in the grated carrots and chopped walnuts (if using) until evenly distributed.
Pour the batter into the prepared cake pan and bake for 35-40 minutes, or until a toothpick inserted into the center of the cake comes out clean.
Let the cake cool in the pan for 5-10 minutes before transferring it to a wire rack to cool completely.
Once the cake has cooled, spread the vegan cream cheese frosting on top and decorate with additional chopped walnuts, if desired.

Vegan Cream Cheese Frosting:
1/2 cup vegan butter, softened
1/2 cup vegan cream cheese, softened
2 cups powdered sugar
1 tsp vanilla extract

Instructions:
In a large bowl, cream together the vegan butter and cream cheese until light and fluffy.
Add the powdered sugar and vanilla extract, and beat until smooth.
If the frosting is too thick, add a splash of almond milk to thin it out.
Spread the frosting on top of the cooled carrot cake and enjoy!

Guacamole Toast

- ripe avocados.
- Juice of 1 lime.
- 1/2 tsp. kosher salt.
- 1/2 c. cherry tomatoes, quartered.
- 1/2. small red onion, minced.
- 1/2. jalapeño, minced.
- clove garlic, minced.
- slices sourdough bread, toasted.

To make the guacamole, start by mashing the ripe avocados in a bowl. Add the juice of one lime and 1/2 teaspoon of kosher salt. Gently mix in the cherry tomatoes, red onion, jalapeño, and garlic. Serve your freshly made guacamole with slices of toasted sourdough bread for a delicious snack! Enjoy!

For an extra flavor boost, try adding diced mango or cilantro! The possibilities are endless! Whatever combination you choose will be sure to add some pizzazz to your homemade guacamole. Experiment away and share your creations with friends and family!

Happy snacking!

Broccoli Cheddar Quinoa Cups

Ingredients:

1 cup cooked quinoa
1 cup cooked and chopped broccoli florets
1 cup shredded cheddar cheese
2 eggs
1/4 cup milk (you can use regular milk or a plant-based alternative)
1/4 teaspoon garlic powder
Salt and pepper to taste

Instructions:

Preheat your oven to 375°F (190°C). Grease or line a mini muffin tin with paper liners.
In a large bowl, combine the cooked quinoa, chopped broccoli, shredded cheddar cheese, eggs, milk, garlic powder, salt, and pepper. Mix well until all the ingredients are evenly incorporated.
Spoon the quinoa mixture into the prepared mini muffin tin, filling each cup about 3/4 full.
Bake in the preheated oven for approximately 15-20 minutes, or until the quinoa cups are set and golden brown on top.
Remove the quinoa cups from the oven and let them cool in the tin for a few minutes. Then transfer them to a wire rack to cool completely.

Optional variations:

You can add other finely chopped vegetables like carrots or bell peppers to the quinoa mixture for added nutrients and flavor.
If your toddler enjoys herbs, you can add some chopped fresh herbs like parsley or dill to enhance the taste.
These broccoli cheddar quinoa cups make a nutritious and tasty snack or meal option for toddlers. They are packed with protein, fiber, and calcium from the quinoa, broccoli, and cheese. Enjoy!

Piccolo Tomato & Basil Risotto

Ingredients:

1/2 cup Arborio rice (risotto rice)
1 cup vegetable broth (low sodium and no added salt)
1/4 cup finely chopped tomatoes
1 tablespoon finely chopped fresh basil
1 tablespoon olive oil
Pinch of garlic powder (optional)
Pinch of salt (optional, if suitable for your baby's age)

Instructions:

In a small saucepan, heat the olive oil over medium heat.
Add the Arborio rice to the saucepan and stir to coat the rice with the oil. Cook for about 1-2 minutes, stirring occasionally.
Gradually add the vegetable broth to the saucepan, about 1/4 cup at a time, stirring constantly. Allow the liquid to be absorbed before adding more. Continue this process until the rice is cooked and has a creamy consistency (around 15-20 minutes).
Add the finely chopped tomatoes, fresh basil, and pinch of garlic powder (if using) to the risotto. Stir to incorporate the ingredients.
If desired, add a pinch of salt (if suitable for your baby's age) to enhance the flavor. Remember that babies under one year old should have minimal added salt in their diet.
Remove the risotto from the heat and let it cool slightly.
Serve the Piccolo Tomato & Basil Risotto to your baby in age-appropriate portions.

This Piccolo Tomato & Basil Risotto is a flavorful and nutritious meal option for your little one. The combination of tomatoes and basil adds a fresh taste, while the Arborio rice provides a creamy texture. Remember to always supervise your baby while they are eating and introduce new foods one at a time to watch for any potential allergies or sensitivities.
Enjoy watching your baby enjoy this delicious risotto!

Veggie Frittata Muffins

Ingredients:

4 large eggs
1/4 cup whole milk or unsweetened plant-based milk
1/2 cup finely chopped mixed vegetables (such as bell peppers, spinach, tomatoes, or broccoli)
1/4 cup grated cheese (cheddar, mozzarella, or a mild cheese of your choice)
1/4 teaspoon dried herbs (such as oregano, basil, or parsley)
Pinch of salt and pepper
Cooking spray or olive oil for greasing

Instructions:

Preheat your oven to 375°F (190°C) and grease a muffin tin with cooking spray or olive oil.
In a mixing bowl, whisk together the eggs and milk until well combined.
Add the finely chopped mixed vegetables, grated cheese, dried herbs, salt, and pepper to the egg mixture. Stir everything together until evenly distributed.
Pour the mixture into the greased muffin tin, filling each cup about 3/4 full.
Bake in the preheated oven for about 15-18 minutes or until the frittata muffins are set and lightly golden on top.
Once baked, remove the muffin tin from the oven and let the frittata muffins cool for a few minutes.
Gently remove the frittata muffins from the muffin tin and let them cool completely on a wire rack.
Cut the Veggie Frittata Muffins into age-appropriate sizes for your baby.

Salmon & Veggie Bites

Ingredients:

1 cup cooked salmon, flaked (you can use canned salmon or cooked fresh salmon)
1/2 cup grated zucchini
1/4 cup grated carrot
1/4 cup whole wheat breadcrumbs or oat flour
1 small egg, beaten
1 tablespoon chopped fresh dill (optional)
1/4 teaspoon garlic powder (optional)
Cooking oil for frying

Instructions:

In a mixing bowl, combine the cooked salmon, grated zucchini, grated carrot, whole wheat breadcrumbs or oat flour, chopped fresh dill (if using), and garlic powder (if using). Mix everything together until well combined.
Add the beaten egg to the mixture and mix again until the ingredients are evenly distributed and the mixture holds together.
Take small portions of the mixture and shape them into small patties or bites that are suitable for your baby's age and preference.
Heat a non-stick skillet or frying pan over medium heat and add a small amount of cooking oil
Place the salmon and veggie bites in the skillet and cook for about 3-4 minutes on each side, or until they are cooked through and golden brown.
Once cooked, remove the bites from the skillet and let them cool slightly.
Cut the salmon and veggie bites into age-appropriate sizes for your baby.
These Salmon & Veggie Bites are a nutritious and flavorful option for your little one. The combination of salmon, grated zucchini, and grated carrot provides protein, omega-3 fatty acids, and a variety of vitamins and minerals. Remember to always supervise your baby while they are eating and introduce new foods one at a time to watch for any potential allergies or sensitivities.

Yogurt & Frozen Blueberries

Ingredients:

1 cup plain Greek yogurt
1/2 cup frozen blueberries

Instructions:

In a small bowl or cup, scoop the Greek yogurt.
Sprinkle the frozen blueberries over the yogurt.
Stir gently to combine, ensuring that the blueberries are evenly distributed throughout the yogurt.
Let the mixture sit for a few minutes to allow the frozen blueberries to thaw slightly and release their juices, which will naturally sweeten the yogurt.
Serve the yogurt and frozen blueberries as is, or you can refrigerate it for a short time to chill if desired.
Optional variations:
You can add a sprinkle of granola or crushed nuts for added texture and crunch.
For added sweetness, you can drizzle a small amount of honey or maple syrup over the yogurt and blueberries.
This recipe is quick, easy, and provides a healthy dose of protein, calcium, and antioxidants from the Greek yogurt and blueberries. It makes a refreshing snack or a nutritious addition to breakfast.
Enjoy!

No-Bake Oatmeal Energy Balls

Ingredients:

1 cup rolled oats
1/2 cup nut or seed butter (such as peanut butter, almond butter, or sunflower seed butter)
1/4 cup honey or maple syrup
1/4 cup ground flaxseed
1/4 cup mini chocolate chips or raisins (optional)
1/2 teaspoon vanilla extract

Instructions:

In a large bowl, combine the rolled oats, nut or seed butter, honey or maple syrup, ground flaxseed, mini chocolate chips or raisins (if using), and vanilla extract.
Mix well until all the ingredients are thoroughly combined. The mixture should be sticky and hold together when pressed.\
If the mixture seems too dry, you can add a little more nut or seed butter or honey/maple syrup. If it's too wet, add more oats or ground flaxseed.
Once the mixture is well combined, portion it out and roll it into small bite-sized balls using your hands.
Place the oatmeal energy balls on a tray or plate lined with parchment paper.
Once all the mixture is rolled into balls, refrigerate them for at least 30 minutes to allow them to firm up.
Optional variations:
You can add shredded coconut, chopped nuts, or dried fruits like cranberries or apricots for added texture and flavor.
For a boost of nutrition, you can incorporate chia seeds or hemp seeds into the mixture.
These no-bake oatmeal energy balls are a nutritious and convenient snack for toddlers. They are packed with fiber, healthy fats, and natural sweetness. Enjoy!

Apple Tart

225g/8oz Odlums Cream Plain Flour.
125g/4oz Butter or Margarine.
¼pt/150ml Cold Water (approx)
4 large Cooking Apples, peeled, cored and sliced.
Sugar, to sweeten apples.
Icing Sugar, to dust (optional)

Instructions for Apple Tart:

Preheat the oven to 190°C/375°F/Gas 5.
Rub the butter into the flour until it resembles breadcrumbs.
Add just enough cold water to bring the pastry together, but not too wet.
Roll out the pastry on a floured surface until it is large enough to cover a 20cm/8" round tart tin.
Line the tin with the pastry, trimming the edges and using a fork to prick the base.
Slice the apples and sweeten with sugar to taste. Arrange the apple slices on top of the pastry base.
Bake the apple tart in the preheated oven for about 30-35 minutes, until the pastry is golden brown and the apples are soft.
Allow the tart to cool before removing it from the tin.
Dust with icing sugar, if desired, before serving.

Yogurt Muffins

Ingredients

2 cups (275g) good quality flour.
2 tsp. baking powder.
1/2 tsp baking soda.
pinch of salt.
1/2 cup (100g) sugar.
2 eggs.
1/2 cup (100ml) light olive oil.
1 cup (250ml) unsweetened yogurt (if using Greek yogurt, add 1 tbsp milk or buttermilk)

We all know how difficult it is to find healthy dessert recipes for kids. But, that doesn't mean you can't make delicious treats that are both tasty and nutritious! These Yogurt Muffins are sure to be a hit with the entire family.

To prepare these muffins, start by preheating your oven to 350°F (180°C). In a large bowl, combine the flour, baking powder, baking soda, and salt. In a separate bowl, mix together the sugar, eggs and oil. Add this mixture to the dry ingredients in the other bowl and stir until just combined.

Now add the yogurt and fold into the batter until it's just combined. Lightly grease a muffin tin and fill each cup with the batter. Bake for 18-20 minutes, or until a toothpick inserted into the center comes out clean. Let cool before serving.

These Yogurt Muffins are a great healthy dessert option that your kids will love! Enjoy!

Cheesy Ham And Broccoli Pasta

Ingredients

1 head of broccoli, cut into small florets.
1 tbsp oil.
1 onion, finely chopped.
2 garlic cloves, crushed.
250g ham, cut into chunks (get a nice thick slice from the deli counter)
300ml pot double cream.
1 tbsp English mustard.

This delicious cheesy ham and broccoli pasta dish is the perfect meal to make for your family, especially if you have young children! It's an easy-to-make recipe that has plenty of flavor and is sure to become a family favorite. To start, heat the oil in a large frying pan over medium heat. Add the chopped onion, garlic and ham and cook for 5 minutes until the vegetables are softened. Then, add the broccoli florets and cook for a further 3-4 minutes. Once the vegetables are cooked, pour in the double cream and mustard and stir together to combine. Allow it to simmer gently for 10 minutes before adding grated cheese of your choice (we recommend cheddar or mozzarella). Once the cheese is melted, turn off the heat and season with salt and pepper to taste. Serve over your favorite cooked pasta noodles and enjoy! With this delicious recipe, your kids will be begging for seconds in no time!

Chicken Pasta Bake

Ingredients
4 tbsp olive oil
1 onion, finely chopped
2 garlic cloves, crushed
¼ tsp chilli flakes
2 x 400g cans chopped tomatoes
1 tsp caster sugar
6 tbsp mascarpone
4 skinless chicken breasts, sliced into strips
300g penne
70g mature cheddar, grated
50g grated mozzarella
½ small bunch of parsley, finely chopped!

Make delicious meals for your kids with this easy-to-follow chicken pasta bake recipe. Begin by preheating the oven to 200°C/ 180°C fan/ gas mark 6. Then, heat 2 tablespoons of olive oil in a large saucepan over a medium heat and add the chopped onion, garlic cloves and chilli flakes. Cook for 5-7 minutes until softened, stirring occasionally.

Add the chopped tomatoes and caster sugar to the pan and bring to a simmer over a medium-high heat. Simmer for about 10 minutes, stirring occasionally until thickened. Add the mascarpone and stir until melted into the tomato sauce.

Heat 2 more tablespoons of olive oil in a separate large saucepan over a medium-high heat. Add the sliced chicken and cook for 5-7 minutes until golden and cooked through, stirring occasionally.

Meanwhile, cook the penne in boiling salted water according to the packet instructions until just al dente. Drain well.

Add the cooked chicken to the tomato sauce and stir to combine. Add the cooked penne, grated cheddar and mozzarella and chopped parsley, season with salt and black pepper, then stir until evenly combined.

Transfer the chicken pasta bake mixture to an ovenproof dish, cover with foil and bake for 20 minutes until bubbling. Remove the foil and bake for a further 5 minutes until the cheese is golden and melted. Serve hot. Enjoy!

Easy Vegan Noodle

Ingredients:

8 oz of noodles of your choice (such as spaghetti or udon)
1/2 cup chopped mushrooms
1/2 cup chopped carrots
1/2 cup chopped red bell pepper
1/2 cup chopped green onions
2 cloves garlic, minced
1/4 cup soy sauce
1 tablespoon sesame oil
1 tablespoon rice vinegar
1 tablespoon maple syrup
1 teaspoon ginger paste
1 teaspoon cornstarch
Salt and black pepper, to taste

Instructions:

Cook the noodles according to the package instructions. Drain and set aside.
In a small bowl, whisk together the soy sauce, sesame oil, rice vinegar, maple syrup, ginger paste, cornstarch, salt, and pepper.
In a large skillet, heat some oil over medium-high heat. Add the chopped mushrooms, carrots, and red bell pepper. Cook for 5-7 minutes or until the vegetables are tender.
Add the minced garlic and cook for an additional minute, stirring constantly.
Add the chopped green onions and the soy sauce mixture to the skillet. Cook for 2-3 minutes or until the sauce thickens.
Add the cooked noodles to the skillet and toss to coat with the sauce.
Serve hot and enjoy!

This vegan noodle dish is quick and easy to make, and it's packed with flavor and nutrients. You can customize the recipe by using your favorite type of noodles and vegetables. It's a great option for a weeknight dinner or a quick lunch.

Peanut Butter Pancakes

Ingredients

250g crunchy peanut butter.
50g unsalted butter, cubed, plus extra for cooking.
6 tbsp maple syrup.
300g self-raising flour.
1 tsp baking powder.
1 tbsp golden caster sugar.
2 large eggs.
350ml milk.

1. In a medium saucepan, melt the peanut butter and butter over low-medium heat until completely combined.
2. Add in the maple syrup, stirring frequently until fully incorporated. Set aside to cool slightly.
3. Combine the flour, baking powder and sugar in a large bowl and stir to combine.
4. In a separate bowl whisk together the eggs and milk until light and frothy, then add this to the dry ingredients along with the cooled peanut butter mixture. Stir together until just combined; don't over mix as this will make your pancakes tough!
5. Heat a non-stick frying pan over medium heat and lightly grease

Sweet Potato Fries

Ingredients:

2 medium sweet potatoes
2 tablespoons olive oil
1/2 teaspoon garlic powder
1/2 teaspoon paprika
1/4 teaspoon salt
1/4 teaspoon black pepper

Instructions:

Preheat your oven to 425°F (220°C). Line a baking sheet with parchment paper or silicone baking mat.
Wash and peel the sweet potatoes. Cut them into thin, evenly sized strips, resembling the shape of fries.
Place the sweet potato fries in a large bowl. Drizzle the olive oil over the fries and sprinkle with garlic powder, paprika, salt, and black pepper.
Toss the sweet potato fries gently in the bowl until they are evenly coated with the seasonings.
Arrange the fries in a single layer on the prepared baking sheet, ensuring they are not overcrowded. This allows them to cook evenly and become crispy.
Bake in the preheated oven for about 20-25 minutes, flipping the fries halfway through the cooking time. The fries should be golden brown and crispy on the outside.
Remove from the oven and let the sweet potato fries cool for a few minutes before serving.

Optional variations:

You can experiment with different seasonings like chili powder, cumin, or dried herbs to customize the flavor of the sweet potato fries.
Serve the fries with a dipping sauce such as ketchup, Greek yogurt, or a homemade honey mustard sauce.
These sweet potato fries are a healthier alternative to regular fries and provide toddlers with a good source of fiber, vitamins, and minerals. Enjoy!

Healthy Banana Cookies

Ingredients:

2 ripe bananas, mashed
1 1/2 cups rolled oats
1/4 cup unsweetened applesauce
1/4 cup nut or seed butter (such as peanut butter, almond butter, or sunflower seed butter)
1/4 cup honey or maple syrup
1 teaspoon vanilla extract
Optional add-ins: raisins, chopped nuts, mini chocolate chips, or dried fruits

Instructions:

Preheat your oven to 350°F (175°C). Line a baking sheet with parchment paper.
In a large bowl, combine the mashed bananas, rolled oats, applesauce, nut or seed butter, honey or maple syrup, and vanilla extract. Stir until all the ingredients are well combined.
If desired, add any optional add-ins such as raisins, chopped nuts, mini chocolate chips, or dried fruits. Stir to incorporate them evenly into the dough.
Drop spoonfuls of the dough onto the prepared baking sheet, spacing them a few inches apart. You can flatten them slightly with the back of a spoon if desired.
Bake in the preheated oven for approximately 12-15 minutes, or until the cookies are lightly golden brown.
Remove from the oven and let the cookies cool on the baking sheet for a few minutes. Then transfer them to a wire rack to cool completely.
Optional variations:
For extra flavor, you can add a pinch of ground cinnamon or nutmeg to the dough.
If your toddler enjoys the taste of coconut, you can add shredded coconut to the dough for added texture and flavor.
These healthy banana cookies are a nutritious and delicious snack for toddlers. They are free from refined sugars and provide natural sweetness from the ripe bananas and honey/maple syrup. Enjoy!

Green Smoothie

Ingredients

Milk- 1 1/2 cup of milk, or any nut milk.
Spinach- 2 cups fully packed.
Banana- 1 banana (frozen is best)
Apple- 1 apple sliced into pieces.
Avocado- 1/4 avocado.

Green smoothies are a healthy and delicious breakfast option for kids. Preparing this nutrient-packed treat is easy – add all of the ingredients to a blender, blend until creamy, and serve!

To make your green smoothie, start by gathering 1 1/2 cups of milk (or any nut milk), 2 cups fully packed spinach, 1 banana (frozen is best), 1 apple sliced into pieces, and 1/4 avocado. Place these ingredients into a blender, and blend until the mixture reaches a creamy consistency. It's now ready to serve!

This healthy breakfast choice is filled with essential vitamins such as vitamin A from spinach and healthy fats from avocado. Not only will it provide lasting energy for your

Baked Feta Pasta

ingredients

2 pints (20 oz) grape tomatoes.
1/2 cup extra-virgin olive oil.
Salt and freshly ground black pepper.
7 oz. block feta cheese (sheep's milk variety), drained.
10 oz. dry pasta (bite size)
5 medium garlic cloves, peeled and halved.
8 oz. ...
1/4 tsp crushed red pepper flakes, or more to taste.

Baked Feta Pasta is an easy and healthy dish that takes only minimal time to prepare. With just a handful of simple ingredients, you can create this delicious meal. To make it, start by preheating your oven to 425 degrees Fahrenheit.

In a large bowl, combine the grape tomatoes, extra-virgin olive oil, salt and pepper. Cut the feta cheese into small cubes and add it to the bowl. Next, cook 10 oz of bite-size pasta according to package instructions until al dente. Once done, drain it and mix it with the tomato mixture in the bowl.

Add garlic cloves, 8 oz of mushrooms (sliced), and 1/4 tsp of crushed red pepper flakes, or to taste. Toss everything together and spread it in a single layer on an oven-safe dish. Bake for 25 minutes until the top is lightly golden brown.

Baked Feta Pasta is now ready to enjoy! Serve with a sprinkling of fresh herbs, extra olive oil, and a side of crusty bread. This healthy pasta dish makes for a great weeknight dinner that is sure to please the whole family. Enjoy!

Creamy Chicken Pasta

Ingredients
500 g | 1lb large chicken breasts (or skinless boneless thighs)
Salt and pepper, to season.
1/2 tbsp olive oil, to fry the chicken.
1 tbsp unsalted butter.
3 garlic cloves, minced.
500 ml | 2 cups double / heavy cream (or you can use single cream)
50 g | ½ cup freshly grated Parmesan cheese.
1 tsp salt.

For delicious recipes for kids, try this Creamy Chicken Pasta! It's easy to make and takes less than 30 minutes. Start by seasoning the chicken breasts with salt and pepper. Heat oil in a large skillet over medium-high heat, then add the chicken breast. Cook until it turns golden brown on both sides, about 4 minutes per side. Once cooked, remove the chicken and set aside. In the same pan, melt butter over medium heat and add minced garlic. Cook for 1 minute until fragrant. Pour in the cream and bring it to a simmer before adding Parmesan cheese and salt. Stir everything together until combined, then add the cooked chicken back in the pan. Reduce heat to low and simmer for 10 minutes, stirring occasionally. Serve over cooked pasta of your choice and enjoy! With this delicious recipe, you can easily delight even the pickiest of eaters. Bon appetite!

Banana & Carrot Bread

Ingredients:

1 ripe banana, mashed
1/2 cup grated carrot
1/4 cup unsweetened applesauce
1/4 cup coconut oil or unsalted butter, melted
1/4 cup pure maple syrup or honey
1/2 cup whole wheat flour
1/2 cup oat flour (you can make it by grinding rolled oats in a blender or food processor)
1/2 teaspoon baking powder
1/4 teaspoon baking soda
1/2 teaspoon ground cinnamon (optional)
Pinch of salt

Instructions:

Preheat your oven to 350°F (175°C) and grease a loaf pan with cooking oil or line it with parchment paper.
In a mixing bowl, combine the mashed banana, grated carrot, unsweetened applesauce, melted coconut oil or unsalted butter, and pure maple syrup or honey. Mix everything together until well combined.
In a separate bowl, whisk together the whole wheat flour, oat flour, baking powder, baking soda, ground cinnamon (if using), and salt.
Gradually add the dry ingredients to the wet ingredients, stirring until just combined. Be careful not to overmix.
Pour the batter into the greased loaf pan and spread it evenly.
Bake in the preheated oven for about 30-35 minutes or until a toothpick inserted into the center comes out clean.
Once baked, remove the bread from the oven and let it cool in the pan for a few minutes.
Transfer the bread to a wire rack and let it cool completely before slicing.
Cut the Banana & Carrot Bread into age-appropriate pieces for your baby.
This Banana & Carrot Bread is a delicious and nutritious treat for your little one. The combination of ripe banana and grated carrot adds natural sweetness and a boost of vitamins and minerals. The whole wheat and oat flours provide fiber, making it a wholesome option. Remember to always supervise your baby while they are eating and introduce new foods one at a time to watch for any potential allergies or sensitivities. Enjoy!

Baked Veggie Frittata Wedges

Ingredients:

4 large eggs
1/4 cup whole milk or unsweetened plant-based milk
1/2 cup finely chopped mixed vegetables (spinach, bell peppers, zucchini, mushrooms, etc.)
1/4 cup grated cheese (cheddar, mozzarella, or a mild cheese of your choice)
1 tablespoon chopped fresh herbs (such as parsley or basil)
Salt and pepper to taste
Cooking spray or olive oil for greasing

Instructions:

Preheat your oven to 375°F (190°C) and grease a square baking dish or line it with parchment paper.
In a mixing bowl, whisk together the eggs and milk until well combined.
Add the finely chopped mixed vegetables, grated cheese, chopped fresh herbs, salt, and pepper to the egg mixture. Stir everything together until evenly distributed.
Pour the mixture into the greased baking dish, spreading it out evenly.
Bake in the preheated oven for about 15-20 minutes or until the frittata is set and lightly golden on top.
Once baked, remove the frittata from the oven and let it cool in the dish for a few minutes.
Cut the frittata into small wedges or squares that are suitable for your baby's age and preference.
Serve the Baked Veggie Frittata Wedges as a standalone meal or as a finger food.
These Baked Veggie Frittata Wedges are a nutritious and versatile option for your little one. They are packed with vegetables, protein from the eggs, and the cheese adds a delightful flavor. You can customize the vegetables and herbs based on your baby's preferences and what's available.
Remember to always supervise your baby while they are eating and introduce new foods one at a time to watch for any potential allergies or sensitivities. Enjoy!

Fruit and Nut Bars

Ingredients:

1 cup rolled oats
1/2 cup dried fruits (such as raisins, cranberries, apricots, or dates), chopped
1/2 cup mixed nuts, chopped (such as almonds, walnuts, or cashews)
1/4 cup honey or maple syrup
1/4 cup peanut butter or almond butter
1/2 teaspoon vanilla extract
Pinch of salt

Instructions:

Preheat your oven to 350°F (175°C) and line a baking dish with parchment paper or lightly grease it with cooking spray.
In a large mixing bowl, combine the rolled oats, dried fruits, and mixed nuts. Mix them together until well combined.
In a small saucepan, heat the honey or maple syrup over low heat until it becomes thin and runny. Remove from heat and stir in the peanut butter or almond butter, vanilla extract, and a pinch of salt. Mix until the mixture is smooth and well combined.
Pour the wet mixture over the dry ingredients in the mixing bowl. Stir well to ensure all the ingredients are evenly coated and combined.
Transfer the mixture to the prepared baking dish and press it down firmly with the back of a spoon or your hands to create an even layer.
Bake in the preheated oven for about 15-20 minutes, or until the edges turn golden brown.
Remove from the oven and allow the bars to cool completely in the baking dish. Once cooled, cut into bars or squares.
These Fruit and Nut Bars can be stored in an airtight container at room temperature for up to a week. They make a great grab-and-go breakfast option for kids or a healthy snack throughout the day. Enjoy!

Delicious Broccoli Soup

Ingredients:

1 head of broccoli, chopped into florets
1 onion, chopped
2 cloves of garlic, minced
1 tablespoon olive oil
4 cups vegetable broth
1/2 teaspoon ground cumin
1/4 teaspoon ground turmeric
Salt and pepper to taste
1/2 cup coconut milk
2 tablespoons nutritional yeast (optional)

Instructions:

In a large pot, heat the olive oil over medium heat.
Add the chopped onion and minced garlic to the pot and sauté until soft and translucent.
Add the chopped broccoli to the pot and stir well to combine with the onions and garlic.
Add the vegetable broth, ground cumin, ground turmeric, salt, and pepper to the pot and bring to a boil.
Reduce the heat to low and let the soup simmer for about 20 minutes, or until the broccoli is tender.
Use an immersion blender or transfer the soup to a blender and blend until smooth and creamy.
Stir in the coconut milk and nutritional yeast (if using).
Adjust the seasoning to taste, adding more salt, pepper, cumin, or turmeric as needed.
Serve hot with crusty bread or crackers on top, and enjoy!

Bolognese Pasta

Ingredients:

1 pound of spaghetti or pasta of your choice
1 large onion, chopped
3 garlic cloves, minced
2 carrots, finely chopped
2 celery stalks, finely chopped
1 red bell pepper, chopped
1 can (28 ounces) of crushed tomatoes
1 can (15 ounces) of tomato sauce
1 tablespoon of tomato paste
1 teaspoon of dried oregano
1 teaspoon of dried basil
1 teaspoon of dried thyme
1 teaspoon of salt
1/2 teaspoon of black pepper
2 tablespoons of olive oil
1/4 cup of chopped fresh parsley
Vegan Parmesan cheese for serving (optional)

Instructions:

Cook the pasta according to package instructions until al dente. Drain the pasta and set it aside.
In a large pot or Dutch oven, heat the olive oil over medium-high heat. Add the onion and sauté for 3-4 minutes, or until the onion is translucent.
Add the garlic, carrots, celery, and red bell pepper to the pot. Cook for 5-7 minutes or until the vegetables are tender.
Add the crushed tomatoes, tomato sauce, tomato paste, dried oregano, dried basil, dried thyme, salt, and black pepper to the pot. Stir well to combine.
Bring the sauce to a boil, then reduce the heat to low and let it simmer for 20-25 minutes, stirring occasionally.
Once the sauce has thickened and the vegetables are tender, add the chopped fresh parsley and stir well.
Serve the sauce over the cooked pasta and top with vegan Parmesan cheese (if using). Enjoy your delicious vegan bolognese pasta!

Shrimps Alfredo Pasta

Shrimp Alfredo pasta is a delicious and easy recipe to make for kids. It's quick, delicious, and full of flavor! To start, you'll need to gather all the necessary ingredients: Fettuccine pasta, shrimp (I used frozen raw 31-40 count per pound size shrimp; you can use smaller or larger), butter (unsalted), cream cheese (for added texture and tangy taste), heavy cream, chicken broth (for added flavor), garlic, and Parmesan cheese.

Once you have all of the ingredients ready to go, start by cooking the fettuccine pasta according to package instructions. Once cooked, drain and set aside. In a large skillet or pan, heat butter over medium-high heat. Add the shrimp to the skillet and cook for 3-5 minutes or until they turn pink. Next, add in the garlic and sauté for 2 minutes. Add in cream cheese, heavy cream, and chicken broth and mix everything together until well combined. Lastly, add in the cooked fettuccine pasta and stir for 1-2 minutes until everything is well incorporated. Serve the delicious Shrimp Alfredo pasta with a generous helping of freshly grated Parmesan cheese. Enjoy!

This delicious Shrimp Alfredo pasta recipe is sure to please the whole family, kids included! It's an easy and delicious way to show your family how much you care. Plus, it's a great way to teach kids how to cook delicious recipes for themselves. So what are you waiting for? Give this delicious Shrimp Alfredo pasta recipe a try today!

Chocolate Chia Pudding

Ingredients

1 14-ounce can light coconut milk.
5 tablespoons chia seeds.
1 tablespoon honey use maple syrup to make vegan.
1/2 teaspoon pure vanilla extract.
Tiny pinch kosher salt.
Toppings of choice fresh fruit, jam, nuts—see blog post for even more ideas!

Chia pudding is a no-sugar dessert recipe that's healthy and easy to prepare. All you need are five ingredients: a 14 ounce can of light coconut milk, 5 tablespoons of chia seeds, 1 tablespoon of honey (replace with maple syrup for vegan diets), 1/2 teaspoon of pure vanilla extract, and a tiny pinch of Kosher salt. To customize your chia pudding, you can also add toppings like fresh fruit, jam, or nuts—check out the blog post for even more ideas! With no added sugar and no cooking time required, this vegan-friendly chia pudding recipe is perfect for a quick healthy dessert. And with plenty of ingredients available at the grocery store, you can whip up a no-sugar dessert in no time! Give it a try today!

Almond Banana Muffins

BANANA muffins Ultra-fine Almond Flour -
Salt
Baking Powder or use 1 teaspoon of baking soda instead.
Cinnamon
Mashed Bananas - the best are ripe bananas to add lots of banana flavor and avoid adding any sweetener in the recipe.
Large Eggs at room temperature
Coconut Oil or melted butter
Vanilla Extract
Stevia Drops or 1/3 cup of granulated sweetener of choice

These muffins are so good, you won't even miss the sugar! ripe bananas add natural sweetness and moisture, while almond flour and coconut oil keep them tender and rich.

To make them, simply combine all of the ingredients in a bowl and mix until well combined. Then, spoon the batter into a muffin tin and bake at 350 degrees F for about 20 minutes.

These almond banana muffins are a delicious and healthy dessert option - perfect for those looking for no sugar dessert recipes! If you want to add more sweetness, you can always drizzle with honey or maple syrup. Enjoy!

Plant-based Veggie Croquettes

Ingredients:

1 cup cooked and mashed sweet potatoes
1 cup cooked and mashed chickpeas
1/2 cup finely chopped mixed vegetables
(carrots, peas, corn, bell peppers, etc.)
1/4 cup whole wheat flour or
breadcrumbs
1 tablespoon ground flaxseed (mixed with
3 tablespoons water as an egg substitute)
1 teaspoon dried herbs (such as oregano,
basil, or parsley)
1/4 teaspoon garlic powder
Salt and pepper to taste
Cooking oil for frying

Instructions:

In a mixing bowl, combine the mashed sweet potatoes, mashed chickpeas, finely chopped mixed vegetables, whole wheat flour or breadcrumbs, ground flaxseed mixture (as an egg substitute), dried herbs, garlic powder, salt, and pepper. Mix everything together until well combined.
Take small portions of the mixture and shape them into croquettes or small patties that are suitable for your baby's age and preference.
Heat a non-stick skillet or frying pan over medium heat and add a small amount of cooking oil.
Place the croquettes in the skillet and cook for about 3-4 minutes on each side, or until they are crispy and browned.
Once cooked, remove the croquettes from the skillet and let them cool slightly.
Cut the veggie croquettes into age-appropriate sizes for your baby.
These Plant-based Veggie Croquettes are packed with nutritious ingredients and offer a variety of flavors and textures. They are a great way to introduce different vegetables and plant-based protein to your baby's diet.
Remember to always supervise your baby while they are eating and introduce new foods one at a time to watch for any potential allergies or sensitivities.
You can serve these veggie croquettes as a standalone meal or as a finger food. They can be enjoyed as is or paired with a dip like hummus or a simple tomato sauce. Enjoy!

Apple & Ginger Loaf

Ingredients:

1 cup whole wheat flour
1/2 cup unsweetened applesauce
1/4 cup grated apple (peeled and cored)
2 tablespoons coconut oil (melted)
2 tablespoons pure maple syrup
1 teaspoon ground ginger
1/2 teaspoon baking powder
1/4 teaspoon baking soda
Pinch of salt

Instructions:

Preheat your oven to 350°F (175°C) and grease a loaf pan with cooking oil or line it with parchment paper.
In a mixing bowl, combine the whole wheat flour, ground ginger, baking powder, baking soda, and salt.
In a separate bowl, whisk together the unsweetened applesauce, grated apple, melted coconut oil, and pure maple syrup until well combined.
Pour the wet ingredients into the dry ingredients and stir until just combined. Be careful not to overmix.
Transfer the batter into the greased loaf pan and spread it evenly.
Bake in the preheated oven for about 25-30 minutes or until a toothpick inserted into the center comes out clean.
Once baked, remove the loaf from the oven and let it cool in the pan for a few minutes.
Transfer the loaf to a wire rack and let it cool completely before slicing.
Cut the Apple & Ginger Loaf into age-appropriate pieces for your baby.
This Apple & Ginger Loaf is a flavorful and nutritious treat for your little one. The combination of applesauce, grated apple, and ginger provides a natural sweetness and a hint of spice. Remember to always supervise your baby while they are eating and introduce new foods one at a time to watch for any potential allergies or sensitivities. Enjoy!

Baby Couscous Recipe

Ingredients:

1/2 cup couscous
1 cup low-sodium vegetable or chicken broth
1/4 cup finely chopped vegetables (carrots, peas, corn, zucchini, etc.)
1 tablespoon finely chopped fresh herbs (parsley, cilantro, basil, etc.) (optional)
1 tablespoon olive oil or unsalted butter (optional)

Instructions:

In a small saucepan, bring the vegetable or chicken broth to a boil.
Remove the saucepan from the heat and add the couscous. Stir to combine.
Cover the saucepan and let the couscous sit for about 5 minutes to allow it to absorb the liquid and soften.
While the couscous is resting, you can steam or boil the finely chopped vegetables until they are tender.
Once the couscous is ready, fluff it with a fork to separate the grains.
If desired, add the cooked vegetables, fresh herbs, and olive oil or unsalted butter to the couscous. Mix everything together gently.
Allow the couscous to cool slightly before serving it to your baby.
Serve the baby couscous as a standalone meal or as a side dish. You can offer it to your baby using a spoon or as a finger food, depending on their age and preference.
Note: You can modify this basic recipe by adding other ingredients such as cooked and shredded chicken, cooked lentils, or finely diced fruits like tomatoes or avocados to introduce different flavors and textures to your baby's meal.
Always make sure the food is properly cooked, mashed or chopped into age-appropriate sizes, and at a suitable temperature for your baby. Remember to supervise your baby while they are eating and introduce new foods one at a time to watch for any potential allergies or sensitivities. Enjoy!

Pumpkin Bread

Ingredients:

1 cup canned pumpkin puree (not pumpkin pie filling)
1/4 cup unsweetened applesauce
1/4 cup maple syrup or honey
1/4 cup melted coconut oil or vegetable oil
2 eggs
1 teaspoon vanilla extract
1 1/2 cups whole wheat flour
1 teaspoon baking powder
1/2 teaspoon baking soda
1/2 teaspoon ground cinnamon
1/4 teaspoon ground nutmeg
1/4 teaspoon ground ginger
1/4 teaspoon salt

Instructions:

Preheat your oven to 350°F (175°C). Grease a loaf pan or line it with parchment paper.
In a large mixing bowl, combine the pumpkin puree, applesauce, maple syrup or honey, melted coconut oil or vegetable oil, eggs, and vanilla extract. Whisk together until well combined.
In a separate bowl, whisk together the whole wheat flour, baking powder, baking soda, ground cinnamon, ground nutmeg, ground ginger, and salt.
Gradually add the dry ingredients to the wet ingredients, stirring until just combined. Be careful not to overmix.
Pour the batter into the prepared loaf pan, spreading it evenly.
Bake in the preheated oven for about 45-50 minutes, or until a toothpick inserted into the center of the bread comes out clean.
Remove the loaf pan from the oven and let the pumpkin bread cool in the pan for a few minutes. Then transfer it to a wire rack to cool completely.
Once cooled, slice the pumpkin bread into baby-sized portions and serve.
Note: This pumpkin bread can be stored in an airtight container at room temperature for up to 3 days, or in the refrigerator for up to a week. You can also freeze individual slices for longer storage. Remember to consult with your pediatrician regarding the introduction of new foods to your baby's diet.

Vegan Baked Oats

Ingredients:

2 cups rolled oats
2 cups unsweetened almond milk
2 ripe bananas, mashed
1/4 cup pure maple syrup
1 tsp vanilla extract
1 tsp ground cinnamon
1/2 tsp baking powder
Pinch of salt
1/2 cup chopped nuts (optional)

Instructions:

Preheat your oven to 375°F (190°C).
In a large mixing bowl, combine the rolled oats, almond milk, mashed bananas, maple syrup, vanilla extract, cinnamon, baking powder, and salt.
Mix well until everything is fully combined.
Pour the mixture into a baking dish or a cast-iron skillet.
Sprinkle the chopped nuts on top, if using.
Bake for 30-35 minutes or until the oats are golden brown and crispy on top.
Serve warm and enjoy!
Note: You can also add other toppings like fresh fruit, coconut flakes, or nut butter to make it more delicious.

Avocado Fusilli Pasta

Ingredients

350g fusilli.
2 cloves garlic, peeled.
200g baby spinach.
2 small ripe avocados, halved and stoned.
extra-virgin olive oil, for drizzling.
30g roasted cashews, chopped.
30g roasted almonds, chopped.
a small bunch coriander, chopped.

For healthy and delicious pasta, you can't go wrong with this avocado fusilli recipe! Start by bringing a large pot of salted water to the boil. Add the fusilli and cook until al dente. Meanwhile, in a large pan over medium heat, add some olive oil and garlic cloves. Saute for 5 minutes until fragrant. Add the baby spinach and cook for a few minutes until wilted. When the pasta is cooked, drain it and add to the pan with the spinach mixture. Finally, top with halved avocados, roasted cashews and almonds and chopped coriander. Drizzle with some extra-virgin olive oil for a healthy finish. Serve and enjoy! This healthy pasta dish is sure to become a favorite in your house. With its creamy avocado, crunchy nuts, and delicious flavors from the garlic, spinach and coriander, it's an easy healthy meal that everyone can enjoy. Try this avocado fusilli recipe today!

Mushroom Pasta With Parmesan

Ingredients
8 ounces* short pasta, like penne, rigatoni, or casarecce, plus saved pasta water.
16 ounces baby bella (cremini) mushrooms (or a mix of other types)
1/2 small sweet onion or yellow onion.
4 tablespoons olive oil, divided.
¾ teaspoon kosher salt, divided.
3 tablespoons salted butter, divided.

This healthy mushroom pasta with parmesan is a quick and easy meal that can be made in 30 minutes or less! To prepare this dish, begin by boiling the 8 ounces of short pasta until al dente. Reserve some of the pasta water to use later when making your sauce. While the pasta cooks, heat 2 tablespoons of olive oil in a large skillet. Add in the mushrooms and onion, and season with 1/2 teaspoon of salt. Cook until the vegetables are softened and lightly browned, about 8-10 minutes. Remove from heat and set aside.

In a separate pan, melt 2 tablespoons of butter over medium heat. Once melted, add in the remaining 2 tablespoons of olive oil, and the cooked vegetables. Give everything a good stir to combine. Continue cooking for another 5 minutes or so until the sauce is golden and bubbly. Add in the reserved pasta water, 1/4 teaspoon of kosher salt, and freshly grated parmesan cheese (to taste). Stir to combine, then add in the cooked pasta. Give everything a good stir before serving! Enjoy your healthy mushroom pasta with parmesan hot, topped with extra parmesan cheese and freshly chopped parsley if desired. Bon Appétit!

Baked Rigatoni Pasta

Ingredients

1 pound rigatoni.
1 pound ground Italian sausage.
1 pound 90/10 ground beef.
1 cup diced yellow onion.
4 garlic cloves, minced.
1 (24 ounce) jar marinara sauce or homemade.
1 (24 ounce) can crushed tomatoes.
1 teaspoon kosher salt.

If you're looking for a healthy and hearty pasta dish, look no further than baked rigatoni! This delicious meal is loaded with healthy ingredients like Italian sausage, ground beef, diced onion, garlic and marinara sauce. Plus it comes together in just one pot for easy preparation. Here's how to make this tasty dish:

Begin by preheating the oven to 350°F. Then, bring a large pot of salted water to a boil and add 1 pound of rigatoni. Cook for 8-10 minutes, stirring occasionally until al dente. Drain and set aside.

In a large skillet over medium-high heat, brown the Italian sausage and ground beef until fully cooked, stirring occasionally. Add the diced yellow onion and minced garlic and sauté until softened, about 3-4 minutes.

Transfer the meat mixture to a large baking dish, then add in the marinara sauce/homemade sauce, crushed tomatoes and salt. Stir everything together. Add the drained rigatoni and stir everything together to evenly coat in the sauce.

Cover the dish with aluminum foil and bake for 20 minutes or until bubbling. Remove from oven and let cool for a few minutes before serving. Enjoy!

Quinoa Bites

Ingredients:

1 cup cooked quinoa
1/2 cup finely grated vegetables (such as carrots, zucchini, or broccoli)
1/2 cup shredded cheese (such as cheddar or mozzarella)
2 tablespoons finely chopped fresh herbs (such as parsley or cilantro)
1/4 teaspoon garlic powder (optional, omit if your baby is not yet ready for garlic)
1/4 teaspoon ground cumin
1/4 teaspoon salt
1/8 teaspoon black pepper
2 eggs, lightly beaten

Instructions:

Preheat your oven to 375°F (190°C). Line a baking sheet with parchment paper or lightly grease it with cooking spray.
In a mixing bowl, combine the cooked quinoa, grated vegetables, shredded cheese, fresh herbs, garlic powder (if using), ground cumin, salt, and black pepper. Mix well until all the ingredients are thoroughly combined.
Add the beaten eggs to the quinoa mixture and stir until the ingredients are well incorporated and the mixture holds together.
Using your hands or a spoon, shape the mixture into small bite-sized balls or patties and place them onto the prepared baking sheet.
Bake the quinoa bites in the preheated oven for about 20-25 minutes, or until they are golden brown and firm to the touch.
Once cooked, remove the quinoa bites from the oven and let them cool on a wire rack.
Allow the quinoa bites to cool down to a safe eating temperature before serving them to your baby.
Note: Always make sure the quinoa bites are at a safe eating temperature before serving them to your baby. These bites can be served as a finger food or cut into smaller pieces if needed.

Easy Chocolate Banana Smoothie

Ingredients:

1 ripe banana
1 cup milk (dairy or plant-based)
1 tablespoon cocoa powder
1 tablespoon honey or maple syrup (optional, for added sweetness)
1/2 teaspoon vanilla extract
Ice cubes (optional, for a colder smoothie)

Instructions:

Peel the ripe banana and break it into smaller pieces.
Place the banana, milk, cocoa powder, honey or maple syrup (if using), and vanilla extract in a blender.
Blend on high speed until all the ingredients are well combined and the smoothie is creamy and smooth. If desired, add a few ice cubes and blend again until smooth and chilled.
Taste the smoothie and adjust the sweetness by adding more honey or maple syrup if desired.
Pour the smoothie into a cup or sippy cup and serve immediately.
Optional variations:
You can add a tablespoon of nut or seed butter, such as peanut butter or almond butter, for added creaminess and flavor.
If your toddler enjoys the taste of cinnamon, you can add a pinch of ground cinnamon to the blender for a hint of spice.
This easy chocolate banana smoothie is a delicious and nutritious treat for toddlers. It provides them with vitamins, minerals, and natural sweetness from the banana and optional sweetener.
Enjoy!

Honey Oatmeal No-Bake Energy Bites

Ingredients:

1 cup old-fashioned rolled oats
1/2 cup natural peanut butter or almond butter
1/4 cup honey
1/4 cup ground flaxseed
1/4 cup mini chocolate chips (optional)
1/2 teaspoon vanilla extract
Pinch of salt

Instructions:

In a mixing bowl, combine the rolled oats, peanut butter or almond butter, honey, ground flaxseed, mini chocolate chips (if using), vanilla extract, and salt. Stir until well combined.

Place the mixture in the refrigerator for about 30 minutes to firm up slightly. This will make it easier to form the energy bites.

Once chilled, take small portions of the mixture and roll them into bite-sized balls using your hands. You can adjust the size based on your toddler's preference.

Place the energy bites on a baking sheet lined with parchment paper and refrigerate for at least 1 hour to allow them to set.

Once set, transfer the energy bites to an airtight container and store them in the refrigerator for up to 1 week.

Banana Cream Pie Overnight Oats

Ingredients:

1 ripe banana, mashed
1 cup rolled oats
1 cup milk (dairy or plant-based)
1/4 cup Greek yogurt
2 tablespoons honey or maple syrup
1/2 teaspoon vanilla extract
1/4 teaspoon ground cinnamon
2 tablespoons crushed graham crackers (optional, for topping)
Sliced bananas and additional honey (optional, for garnish)

Instructions:

In a medium-sized bowl, mash the ripe banana with a fork until smooth.
Add the rolled oats, milk, Greek yogurt, honey or maple syrup, vanilla extract, and ground cinnamon to the bowl with the mashed banana. Stir everything together until well combined.
Divide the mixture into individual jars or containers with airtight lids.
Place the jars/containers in the refrigerator and let them sit overnight, or for at least 4 hours, to allow the oats to absorb the liquid and become creamy.
When ready to serve, give the overnight oats a good stir. If desired, top each serving with sliced bananas, a drizzle of honey, and a sprinkle of crushed graham crackers.
Enjoy the Banana Cream Pie Overnight Oats cold from the refrigerator.
These overnight oats are a convenient and nutritious breakfast option for kids. They can be prepared in advance, making busy mornings a little easier. The combination of creamy banana, oats, and a hint of cinnamon creates a delightful flavor reminiscent of banana cream pie.

Vegan Alfredo Pasta

Ingredients:

12 oz (340 g) of fettuccine pasta
1 1/2 cups (360 ml) of unsweetened almond milk
1/2 cup (120 ml) of vegetable broth
1/2 cup (60 g) of nutritional yeast
3 cloves of garlic, minced
2 tbsp (30 ml) of olive oil
2 tbsp (30 ml) of cornstarch
1 tsp (5 ml) of salt
1/4 tsp (1.25 ml) of black pepper
Fresh parsley or basil, chopped, for garnish

Instructions:

Cook the fettuccine pasta according to the package instructions until al dente. Drain and set aside.
In a small bowl, whisk together the almond milk, vegetable broth, nutritional yeast, cornstarch, salt, and black pepper.
In a large skillet, heat the olive oil over medium heat. Add the minced garlic and sauté for 1-2 minutes, or until fragrant.
Pour the almond milk mixture into the skillet with the garlic and whisk continuously for 3-5 minutes, or until the sauce starts to thicken.
Add the cooked fettuccine to the skillet with the sauce and toss until the pasta is fully coated in the sauce.
Continue to cook the pasta and sauce for 2-3 minutes, or until the sauce has thickened and the pasta is heated through.
Divide the pasta alfredo into bowls and garnish with chopped fresh parsley or basil.
Enjoy your delicious vegan pasta alfredo!

Fettuccine Alfredo

Ingredients

227g tub clotted cream.
25g butter (about 2 tbsp)
1 tsp cornflour.
100g parmesan, grated.
freshly grated nutmeg.
250g fresh fettuccine or tagliatelle.
snipped chives or chopped parsley, to serve (optional)
!

Fettuccine Alfredo is a delicious and easy-to-make recipe for kids. It's the perfect dish for family dinners or impressing your friends! Here's how to make it:

1. Start by bringing a large pot of salted water to a boil over medium-high heat.

2. Once the water is boiling, add the fresh fettuccine or tagliatelle and cook for about 8-10 minutes until it's al dente.

3. While the pasta cooks, prepare the sauce: In a separate pan, melt the butter over medium-high heat before adding in the clotted cream. Once combined, add in the cornflour, grated parmesan cheese, and a pinch of nutmeg. Stir until everything is combined.

4. Once the pasta is cooked, drain it and add it to the sauce pan with the sauce ingredients. Stir until the pasta is evenly coated before serving with snipped chives or chopped parsley (optional).

Fettuccine Alfredo is a delicious, easy-to-make recipe for kids and adults alike. Enjoy this delicious dish with family or friends - bon appetit!

Yogurt Cake

Ingredients

1 box sugar-free yellow cake mix (16 oz), or any 15-16 oz box cake mix.
2 individual sized containers (5.3 oz each) nonfat vanilla greek yogurt.
1 cup water.
8 oz container cool whip, optional, for frosting.

This no-sugar dessert recipe is sure to please! An easy and healthy way to get your sweet treat fix without breaking the calorie bank, this yogurt cake is made with just four simple ingredients. Start by preheating your oven to 350 degrees Fahrenheit. In a large bowl, combine the cake mix, Greek yogurt, and water until everything is completely combined and no lumps remain. Grease a 9x13 inch pan and pour in the batter evenly. Bake for 25-30 minutes or until a toothpick inserted into the center of the cake comes out clean. Let cool before frosting with Cool Whip, if desired. Enjoy your delicious no sugar dessert! With this recipe, you can have your cake and eat it too!

This no sugar dessert recipe is a great way to indulge without the guilt. Perfect for parties or just an everyday indulgence, this yogurt cake is sure to be a crowd pleaser. It's so easy to make and no one will ever know that it's sugar-free! Try this no sugar dessert recipe today and enjoy a healthy, delicious treat. Your taste buds will thank you!

Raspberry Smoothie Bowl

Ingredients:

1 cup frozen raspberries
1 ripe banana
1/2 cup Greek yogurt
1/4 cup milk (dairy or plant-based)
1 tablespoon honey or maple syrup (optional, for added sweetness)
Toppings of your choice: sliced fresh fruit, granola, shredded coconut, chia seeds, or honey drizzle

Instructions:

In a blender, combine the frozen raspberries, ripe banana, Greek yogurt, milk, and honey or maple syrup (if using).

Blend the ingredients until smooth and creamy. If needed, add a little more milk to achieve your desired consistency.

Pour the raspberry smoothie into a bowl.

Decorate the smoothie bowl with your favorite toppings. You can arrange sliced fresh fruit, sprinkle granola, add shredded coconut, sprinkle chia seeds, or drizzle a little honey on top.

Serve the Raspberry Smoothie Bowl immediately and enjoy with a spoon.

Smoothie bowls are a fun and nutritious way to start the day. They're packed with vitamins, minerals, and fiber from the fruits, and the Greek yogurt adds protein and creaminess. Letting kids customize their smoothie bowls with their favorite toppings can make breakfast more exciting and interactive.

Vegan Lentil Meatballs

Ingredients:

1 cup (200 g) of dried brown lentils, rinsed and drained
2 cups (480 ml) of vegetable broth
1 small onion, chopped
3 cloves of garlic, minced
2 tbsp (30 ml) of olive oil
1/2 cup (60 g) of bread crumbs
1/4 cup (30 g) of nutritional yeast
1 tbsp (15 ml) of tomato paste
1 tbsp (15 ml) of soy sauce or tamari
1 tsp (5 ml) of dried oregano
1 tsp (5 ml) of dried basil
Salt and black pepper, to taste

Instructions:

In a medium saucepan, combine the rinsed lentils and vegetable broth. Bring the mixture to a boil over high heat, then reduce the heat to low and simmer, covered, for 25-30 minutes, or until the lentils are soft and most of the liquid has been absorbed. Drain off any excess liquid and let the lentils cool.
Preheat the oven to 400°F (200°C) and line a baking sheet with parchment paper.
In a large skillet, heat the olive oil over medium heat. Add the chopped onion and sauté for 2-3 minutes, or until it's soft and translucent. Add the minced garlic and sauté for another 1-2 minutes.
In a large bowl, combine the cooked lentils, sautéed onion and garlic, bread crumbs, nutritional yeast, tomato paste, soy sauce or tamari, dried oregano, dried basil, salt, and black pepper. Mix everything together until well combined.
Using your hands, form the lentil mixture into golf ball-sized balls and place them on the prepared baking sheet. Bake the lentil meatballs for 20-25 minutes, or until they're golden brown and crispy on the outside.
Serve the vegan lentil meatballs with your favorite pasta or grain, and top with your favorite sauce. Enjoy!
Note: These lentil meatballs can also be frozen for later use. Simply place them on a baking sheet and freeze until solid, then transfer them to an airtight container or freezer bag. To reheat, simply bake them in a preheated oven at 400°F (200°C) for 10-15 minutes, or until heated through.

Crispy Quinoa Cakes

Ingredients:

1 cup (180g) uncooked quinoa
2 cups (480 ml) water
1/2 cup (50 g) panko breadcrumbs (or other breadcrumbs of your choice)
1/2 cup (60 g) all-purpose flour
1/4 cup (30 g) nutritional yeast
1/4 cup (60 ml) olive oil
1/4 cup (60 ml) water
2 cloves of garlic, minced
1 small onion, chopped
1 tsp (5 ml) salt
1/2 tsp (2.5 ml) black pepper
1/4 tsp (1.25 ml) cayenne pepper (optional)
Vegetable oil for frying

Instructions:

Rinse the quinoa in a fine-mesh strainer and place it in a medium saucepan with 2 cups of water. Bring the water to a boil over high heat, then reduce the heat to low and simmer, covered, for 15-20 minutes or until the water has been absorbed and the quinoa is tender. Let the quinoa cool.

In a large mixing bowl, combine the cooled quinoa, panko breadcrumbs, all-purpose flour, nutritional yeast, garlic, onion, salt, black pepper, and cayenne pepper (if using). Mix everything together until well combined.
In a separate small bowl, whisk together the olive oil and 1/4 cup of water. Pour this mixture over the quinoa mixture and mix everything together until well combined.
Use your hands to form the quinoa mixture into 2-3 inch (5-7.5 cm) wide patties, about 1/2 inch (1.25 cm) thick.
Heat enough vegetable oil in a large frying pan over medium-high heat. Once the oil is hot, carefully place the quinoa cakes in the pan, making sure not to overcrowd them. Cook for 2-3 minutes on each side, or until golden brown and crispy.
Once cooked, place the quinoa cakes on a paper towel-lined plate to absorb any excess oil.
Serve the crispy quinoa cakes with a side salad or your favorite dipping sauce. Enjoy!
Note: These quinoa cakes can also be baked in the oven at 375°F (190°C) for 20-25 minutes, or until golden brown and crispy.

Ham and Cheese Breakfast Bake

Ingredients:

6 cups cubed bread (such as French bread or ciabatta)
2 cups diced cooked ham
1 1/2 cups shredded cheddar cheese
1 cup shredded mozzarella cheese
1/2 cup diced onion
1/2 cup diced bell pepper (any color)
6 large eggs
2 cups milk (dairy or plant-based)
1 teaspoon Dijon mustard
1/2 teaspoon garlic powder
1/2 teaspoon dried thyme
Salt and pepper, to taste
Chopped fresh parsley, for garnish (optional)

Instructions:

Preheat your oven to 375°F (190°C). Grease a 9x13-inch baking dish with cooking spray or butter.

Spread the cubed bread evenly in the prepared baking dish. Sprinkle the diced ham, cheddar cheese, mozzarella cheese, diced onion, and diced bell pepper over the bread.

In a large bowl, whisk together the eggs, milk, Dijon mustard, garlic powder, dried thyme, salt, and pepper until well combined.

Pour the egg mixture over the bread and toppings in the baking dish. Press down gently with a spatula to make sure the bread is soaked in the liquid.

Cover the baking dish with foil and let it sit at room temperature for about 20-30 minutes to allow the bread to absorb the liquid.

Remove the foil and bake the breakfast bake in the preheated oven for about 35-40 minutes, or until the top is golden brown and the eggs are set.

Remove from the oven and let it cool for a few minutes before serving. Garnish with chopped fresh parsley, if desired.

This Ham and Cheese Breakfast Bake is a satisfying and flavorful dish that's perfect for a leisurely breakfast or brunch. It's packed with ham, cheese, and a medley of savory flavors. You can also customize it by adding your favorite vegetables or herbs. Serve it warm alongside a fresh salad or fruit for a complete meal.

Pumpkin Pie Biscuits

Ingredients:

1 cup canned pumpkin puree (not pumpkin pie filling)
1 1/2 cups whole wheat flour
1/2 teaspoon ground cinnamon
1/4 teaspoon ground nutmeg
1/4 teaspoon ground ginger
1/4 teaspoon baking powder
1/4 teaspoon baking soda
2 tablespoons unsalted butter, melted
1 tablespoon maple syrup or honey (optional)
Cooking spray or additional melted butter for greasing

Instructions:

Preheat your oven to 375°F (190°C). Line a baking sheet with parchment paper or lightly grease it with cooking spray.
In a mixing bowl, combine the pumpkin puree, whole wheat flour, cinnamon, nutmeg, ginger, baking powder, and baking soda. Mix well until all the ingredients are thoroughly combined.
Add the melted butter and maple syrup or honey (if using) to the mixture. Stir until the ingredients are well incorporated and a soft dough forms.
Lightly flour a clean surface and transfer the dough onto it. Roll out the dough to a thickness of about 1/2 inch.
Use a cookie cutter or small cup to cut out biscuit shapes from the dough. Place the cut-out biscuits onto the prepared baking sheet.
Bake the biscuits in the preheated oven for about 12-15 minutes, or until they are golden brown and firm to the touch.
Once cooked, remove the biscuits from the oven and let them cool on a wire rack.
Allow the pumpkin pie biscuits to cool down to a safe eating temperature before serving them to your baby.
Note: Always make sure the biscuits are at a safe eating temperature before serving them to your baby. These biscuits can be served as a snack or a dessert option.

Chocolate Zucchini Muffins

Ingredients:

1 cup all-purpose flour
1/4 cup unsweetened cocoa powder
1/2 teaspoon baking soda
1/4 teaspoon baking powder
1/4 teaspoon salt
1/2 cup granulated sugar
1/4 cup unsalted butter, melted
1/4 cup unsweetened applesauce
1 large egg
1 teaspoon vanilla extract
1 cup grated zucchini (about 1 medium zucchini)
1/2 cup chocolate chips

Instructions:

Preheat your oven to 350°F (175°C). Grease or line a muffin tin with paper liners.
In a medium bowl, whisk together the flour, cocoa powder, baking soda, baking powder, and salt. Set aside.
In a large bowl, whisk together the sugar, melted butter, applesauce, egg, and vanilla extract until well combined.
Add the grated zucchini to the wet ingredients and stir until evenly distributed.
Gradually add the dry ingredients to the wet ingredients, stirring until just combined. Be careful not to overmix.
Gently fold in the chocolate chips.
Scoop the batter into the prepared muffin tin, filling each cup about 2/3 full.
Bake in the preheated oven for approximately 18-22 minutes, or until a toothpick inserted into the center of a muffin comes out clean.
Remove from the oven and let the muffins cool in the tin for a few minutes. Then transfer them to a wire rack to cool completely.
Optional variations:
You can add a 1/2 teaspoon of cinnamon or a pinch of nutmeg for added flavor.
If your toddler enjoys the taste of nuts, you can add a 1/4 cup of chopped walnuts or pecans to the batter.
These chocolate zucchini muffins are a delicious and sneaky way to incorporate vegetables into your toddler's diet. The zucchini adds moisture and nutrients, while the chocolate makes them appealing to little ones. Enjoy!

Scrambled Egg Tacos

Ingredients:

4 large eggs
2 tablespoons milk (dairy or plant-based)
Salt and pepper, to taste
1 tablespoon butter or cooking oil
4 small flour tortillas
Toppings (optional):
Shredded cheese
Salsa
Diced tomatoes
Chopped avocado
Sour cream
Chopped fresh cilantro

Instructions:

In a bowl, whisk together the eggs, milk, salt, and pepper until well combined.
Heat the butter or cooking oil in a non-stick skillet over medium heat.
Pour the egg mixture into the skillet and cook, stirring gently, until the eggs are scrambled and cooked to your desired consistency.
Warm the flour tortillas in a dry skillet or in the microwave for a few seconds, until they are soft and pliable.
Place a portion of the scrambled eggs onto each tortilla, dividing it equally among them.
Add your desired toppings, such as shredded cheese, salsa, diced tomatoes, chopped avocado, sour cream, and fresh cilantro.
Fold the tortillas over the filling, creating a taco shape.
Serve the Scrambled Egg Tacos immediately and enjoy!
These Scrambled Egg Tacos are a delicious and protein-packed breakfast option for kids. The creamy and fluffy scrambled eggs paired with the warm tortillas and customizable toppings make for a satisfying and flavorful meal. Encourage your kids to choose their favorite toppings and let them build their own tacos for a fun and interactive breakfast experience.

Cottage Cheese Pancakes

Ingredients:

1 cup cottage cheese
4 large eggs
1/4 cup all-purpose flour
2 tablespoons sugar or sweetener of your choice
1/2 teaspoon vanilla extract
1/4 teaspoon baking powder
Pinch of salt
Butter or cooking oil for greasing the pan

Optional toppings:

Fresh berries
Maple syrup
Honey
Yogurt

Instructions:

In a blender or food processor, combine the cottage cheese, eggs, flour, sugar, vanilla extract, baking powder, and salt. Blend until smooth and well combined.
Heat a non-stick skillet or griddle over medium heat and lightly grease it with butter or cooking oil.
Pour about 1/4 cup of the pancake batter onto the skillet for each pancake. You can make them as small or as large as you prefer.
Cook the pancakes for about 2-3 minutes, or until the edges start to set and bubbles form on the surface.
Flip the pancakes and cook for another 1-2 minutes, or until golden brown and cooked through.
Remove the pancakes from the skillet and keep them warm. Repeat with the remaining batter, adding more butter or oil to the skillet as needed.
Serve the Cottage Cheese Pancakes with your choice of toppings, such as fresh berries, maple syrup, honey, or a dollop of yogurt.
These Cottage Cheese Pancakes are a nutritious and protein-rich breakfast option for kids. The cottage cheese adds a creamy texture and a boost of protein to the pancakes. Feel free to customize the toppings based on your child's preferences, and serve them with a side of fresh fruit for a complete and delicious meal.

Pesto Pasta

Ingredients

6 ounces spaghetti, reserve 1/2 cup starchy pasta water.
1/3 to 1/2 cup. basil pesto or vegan pesto.
Extra-virgin olive oil, for drizzling.
Fresh lemon juice, as desired.
4 cups arugula.
2 tablespoons pine nuts.
Pinches of red pepper flakes.
Sea salt and freshly ground black pepper.

Cooking delicious recipes for kids doesn't have to be complicated. With the right ingredients, you can make delicious pesto pasta in a flash! To begin, bring a large pot of salted water to a boil and add the spaghetti. Cook according to package instructions until al dente. Reserve 1/2 cup of starchy pasta water before straining.

In a large bowl, mix together the basil pesto, arugula and pine nuts and season with salt, pepper and red pepper flakes to taste. Next, add the cooked spaghetti to the pesto mixture along with a little of the reserved pasta water to thin out the sauce if desired. Drizzle with extra-virgin olive oil and lemon juice, if desired.

Give the delicious pesto pasta a good stir to coat all the ingredients evenly. Plate up and enjoy! This delicious recipe is sure to be a hit with kids of all ages and tastes great as leftovers too. Give it a try today and enjoy some delicious pesto pasta for dinner tonight!

Happy cooking!

Creamy Salmon Pasta

Ingredients
2 salmon fillets.
1 tbsp olive oil, plus 1 tsp if roasting.
175g penne.
2 shallots or 1 small onion, finely chopped.
1 garlic clove, crushed.
100ml white wine.
200ml double cream or crème fraîche.
¼ lemon, zested and juiced.

Creamy salmon pasta is a delicious and easy recipe for kids. This delicious meal can be prepared in just a few simple steps.

To begin, preheat your oven to 200°c (gas mark 6) and brush the salmon fillets with 1 tbsp of olive oil. Place them in the oven to bake for 12-15 minutes until cooked through. Once the salmon is cooked, flake it into small pieces and set aside.

Bring a large pot of salted water to the boil and cook your penne according to packet instructions until al dente.

Meanwhile, heat 1 tsp of olive oil in a large skillet over medium-high heat. Add the shallots or onions and garlic to the skillet and sauté for a few minutes until softened. Add the white wine, cream or crème fraîche, lemon zest, lemon juice and flaked salmon pieces. Simmer gently over low heat for around 5-7 minutes until the sauce has thickened slightly.

To serve, drain the cooked penne and combine with the sauce. Divide into plates and enjoy your delicious creamy salmon pasta!

This delicious recipe is sure to be a hit with all the family - even picky eaters will love it! With only a few simple ingredients, this meal can be prepared in no time at all so why not give it a try tonight? Enjoy!

Peanut Butter and Jelly Muffins

Ingredients:

1 3/4 cups all-purpose flour
1/2 cup granulated sugar
2 1/2 teaspoons baking powder
1/2 teaspoon salt
3/4 cup milk (dairy or plant-based)
1/2 cup creamy peanut butter
1/4 cup unsalted butter, melted
1 large egg
1 teaspoon vanilla extract
1/2 cup jelly or jam of your choice

Instructions:
Preheat your oven to 375°F (190°C). Line a muffin tin with paper liners or grease the cups.
In a large mixing bowl, whisk together the flour, sugar, baking powder, and salt.
In a separate bowl, combine the milk, peanut butter, melted butter, egg, and vanilla extract. Stir until smooth and well combined.
Pour the wet ingredients into the dry ingredients and mix until just combined. Do not overmix; a few lumps are okay.
Spoon a tablespoon of batter into each muffin cup, filling it about one-third of the way.
Add a teaspoonful of jelly or jam on top of the batter in each cup.
Cover the jelly or jam with another tablespoon of batter, filling the cups about two-thirds of the way.
Bake in the preheated oven for 15-18 minutes, or until a toothpick inserted into the center of a muffin comes out clean.
Remove the muffins from the oven and let them cool in the pan for a few minutes. Then transfer them to a wire rack to cool completely.
These Peanut Butter and Jelly Muffins are a delicious twist on the classic sandwich flavors. They are soft, moist, and filled with a sweet surprise of jelly or jam in the center. Pack them as a delightful breakfast treat for kids, or enjoy them as an afternoon snack. These muffins can be stored in an airtight container for a few days. Enjoy the nostalgic flavors of peanut butter and jelly in a convenient and tasty muffin form!

Vegan Banana Fritters

Ingredients:

3 ripe bananas, mashed
1/2 cup (60 g) of all-purpose flour
1/4 cup (30 g) of cornstarch
1/4 cup (50 g) of granulated sugar
1 tsp (5 g) of baking powder
1/4 tsp (1.5 g) of salt
1/4 tsp (0.5 g) of ground cinnamon
1/4 cup (60 ml) of plant-based milk
Vegetable oil, for frying
Powdered sugar, for dusting

Instructions:

In a mixing bowl, combine the mashed bananas, flour, cornstarch, sugar, baking powder, salt, and cinnamon. Mix well until the batter is smooth.
Gradually add the plant-based milk to the batter, stirring until it is well incorporated and smooth.
Heat the vegetable oil in a deep frying pan over medium-high heat. The oil should be hot enough that a small drop of batter sizzles and floats to the surface immediately.
Use a spoon to drop the batter into the hot oil, making small fritters that are about 2-3 inches (5-7.5 cm) in diameter. Fry the fritters in batches, being careful not to overcrowd the pan.
Fry the fritters for about 2-3 minutes on each side, or until they are golden brown and crispy.
Use a slotted spoon to transfer the fritters to a paper towel-lined plate to drain any excess oil.
Repeat the frying process with the remaining batter until all the fritters are cooked.
Dust the crispy banana fritters with powdered sugar before serving.
Enjoy your crispy and sweet vegan banana fritters as a snack or dessert!

Tuna Pasta

Ingredients

2 tablespoons olive oil.
2 large cloves garlic minced.
1 (5 ounce) can tuna, drained I prefer tuna packed in oil.
1 teaspoon lemon juice.
1 tablespoon fresh parsley chopped.
Salt & pepper to taste.
4 ounces uncooked pasta (I used spaghetti)

Tuna pasta is a delicious and easy-to-make recipe for kids. It's perfect for busy weeknights when you don't have much time to cook. To make this delicious dish, start by heating the olive oil in a large skillet over medium heat. Add the garlic and sauté until fragrant, about 1 minute. Add the tuna and stir to combine. Then add the lemon juice and parsley, season with salt and pepper to taste, and cook for another minute or two. Finally, add the uncooked pasta to the skillet and mix everything together. Cook according to directions on the box until al dente. Serve hot and enjoy! Tuna pasta is a delicious and nutritious meal that your kids will love. Enjoy!

Lemon Bars

Healthy Lemon Bars are an easy no-sugar dessert recipe that you can enjoy guilt-free. This delicious treat is made with just 5 simple ingredients and no added sugars, making it a healthy alternative to traditional sugary desserts. With its bright and zesty flavors of lemon juice and zest, this no sugar dessert will surely become a favorite.

To create this no-sugar dessert, start by combining all-purpose flour (or whole wheat or oat flour), butter (or solid coconut oil), granulated sweetener (erythritol, stevia, sugar) and eggs in a bowl until well blended. Press the mixture into a baking pan and bake at 350 degrees Fahrenheit for 20 minutes.

Once the base is baked, combine lemon juice and zest with an additional sweetener of your choice in a bowl and pour it over the top of the cooked layer. Bake for an additional 15 minutes and cool completely before cutting into bars. Serve chilled or at room temperature for a light, no sugar dessert that is sure to satisfy your sweet tooth. Enjoy!

Try this no-sugar dessert recipe today and indulge without the guilt of added sugars. Healthy Lemon Bars are a delicious way to satisfy your sweet cravings in a healthy and satisfying way. With its bright flavors and no added sugar, it's no wonder why this no sugar dessert is a favorite.

Try it today and let us know how you liked it! You won't be disappointed. Enjoy!

Quick Chili Mac

Ingredients:

8 ounces elbow macaroni
1 tablespoon olive oil
1 pound ground beef (or ground turkey or plant-based ground meat substitute)
1 small onion, diced
2 cloves garlic, minced
1 can (15 ounces) kidney beans, drained and rinsed
1 can (14.5 ounces) diced tomatoes
1 can (8 ounces) tomato sauce
1 tablespoon chili powder
1/2 teaspoon cumin
Salt and pepper to taste
Shredded cheddar cheese (optional, for topping)
Chopped green onions or fresh cilantro (for garnish)

Instructions:

Cook the elbow macaroni according to the package instructions until al dente. Drain and set aside.
In a large skillet, heat the olive oil over medium heat. Add the diced onion and minced garlic, and sauté until fragrant and translucent.
Add the ground beef to the skillet and cook until browned and cooked through. If using plant-based ground meat substitute, follow the package instructions for cooking.
Drain any excess grease from the skillet if necessary.
Add the kidney beans, diced tomatoes, tomato sauce, chili powder, cumin, salt, and pepper to the skillet. Stir to combine all the ingredients.
Reduce the heat to low and let the chili mixture simmer for about 10 minutes, allowing the flavors to meld together.
Add the cooked elbow macaroni to the skillet and stir until the pasta is well coated with the chili sauce.
Cook for an additional 2-3 minutes to heat the pasta through.
Optional: Sprinkle shredded cheddar cheese on top of the chili mac and cover the skillet for a minute or two to melt the cheese.
Remove from heat and garnish with chopped green onions or fresh cilantro.
Serve the Quick Chili Mac warm and enjoy!
Note: You can adjust the spiciness of the dish by adding more or less chili powder. If your child prefers milder flavors, you can omit or reduce the amount of chili powder and cumin. Feel free to customize the recipe by adding diced bell peppers, corn, or any other vegetables your child enjoys.

Bacon Breakfast Pizza

Ingredients:

1 pre-made pizza crust or pizza dough
1 cup shredded mozzarella cheese
4 slices cooked bacon, crumbled
4 large eggs
Salt and pepper, to taste
Optional toppings:
Diced bell peppers
Diced onions
Sliced mushrooms
Chopped tomatoes
Sliced black olives

Instructions:

Preheat your oven according to the instructions on the pre-made pizza crust or pizza dough package.
Roll out the pizza crust or dough to your desired thickness on a lightly floured surface. Transfer it to a baking sheet or pizza stone.
Sprinkle the shredded mozzarella cheese evenly over the pizza crust.
Sprinkle the crumbled bacon on top of the cheese.
Create four wells in the cheese and bacon mixture for the eggs. Carefully crack an egg into each well.
Season the eggs with salt and pepper, to taste.
Add any optional toppings of your choice, such as diced bell peppers, onions, mushrooms, tomatoes, or black olives.
Bake the bacon breakfast pizza in the preheated oven according to the instructions on the pizza crust or dough package, or until the cheese is melted and bubbly, and the eggs are cooked to your desired level of doneness.
Remove the pizza from the oven and let it cool for a few minutes.
Slice the pizza into wedges or squares and serve.
This Bacon Breakfast Pizza combines the flavors of a classic breakfast with the convenience of pizza. The crispy bacon adds a savory element, while the eggs provide protein and richness. Customize the pizza with your child's favorite toppings to make it even more enjoyable. It's a great way to start the day with a fun and delicious breakfast.

Egg Bake Breakfast Casserole

Ingredients:

8 large eggs
1 cup milk
1 cup shredded cheddar cheese
1 cup diced ham or cooked bacon
1/2 cup diced bell peppers (any color)
1/2 cup diced onions
1/2 teaspoon salt
1/4 teaspoon black pepper
Cooking spray or butter, for greasing the baking dish

Instructions:

Preheat your oven to 375°F (190°C). Grease a 9x13-inch baking dish with cooking spray or butter.
In a large mixing bowl, whisk together the eggs and milk until well combined.
Add the shredded cheddar cheese, diced ham or cooked bacon, diced bell peppers, diced onions, salt, and black pepper to the bowl. Stir to evenly distribute the ingredients.
Pour the mixture into the greased baking dish, spreading it out evenly.
Bake in the preheated oven for 25-30 minutes, or until the eggs are set and the top is golden brown.
Remove the casserole from the oven and let it cool for a few minutes before serving.
Slice the Egg Bake Breakfast Casserole into squares or rectangles and serve.
This Egg Bake Breakfast Casserole is a hearty and satisfying option for a family breakfast. It's packed with protein from the eggs and ham or bacon, and the bell peppers and onions add a pop of flavor and color. You can customize the casserole by adding other ingredients like spinach, mushrooms, or different types of cheese. This recipe is also great for meal prep, as you can make it ahead of time and reheat slices for a quick breakfast during busy mornings. Enjoy this delicious and nutritious breakfast casserole!

Sweet Potato Pancakes

Ingredients:

1 small sweet potato
1/2 cup all-purpose flour
1/2 teaspoon baking powder
1/4 teaspoon ground cinnamon (optional)
1/4 cup milk (breast milk, formula, or cow's milk)
1 small egg
1 tablespoon unsalted butter, melted
Maple syrup or yogurt (optional, for serving)

Instructions:

Peel the sweet potato and cut it into small chunks. Steam or boil the sweet potato until it becomes soft and tender. Drain and let it cool down.
In a mixing bowl, mash the cooked sweet potato with a fork until it is smooth.
Add the all-purpose flour, baking powder, and ground cinnamon (if using) to the mashed sweet potato. Mix well.
In a separate bowl, whisk together the milk, egg, and melted butter.
Pour the wet ingredients into the sweet potato mixture and stir until well combined. The batter should have a smooth consistency.
Heat a non-stick skillet or griddle over medium heat. Lightly grease it with cooking spray or a small amount of butter.
Spoon small portions of the pancake batter onto the skillet. Cook for 2-3 minutes on each side, or until the pancakes are golden brown.
Remove the pancakes from the skillet and let them cool down slightly before serving.
Serve the sweet potato pancakes as is or drizzle them with a small amount of maple syrup or serve with a dollop of yogurt.

Healthy Strawberry Muffins

Ingredients:

1 and 1/2 cups whole wheat flour
1/2 cup oats
1/2 cup honey or maple syrup
1/4 cup melted coconut oil or vegetable oil
1/4 cup unsweetened applesauce
2 large eggs
1 teaspoon vanilla extract
1 teaspoon baking powder
1/2 teaspoon baking soda
1/4 teaspoon salt
1 cup diced strawberries

Instructions:

Preheat your oven to 350°F (175°C). Grease or line a muffin tin with muffin liners.
In a large mixing bowl, whisk together the whole wheat flour, oats, baking powder, baking soda, and salt.
In a separate bowl, whisk together the honey or maple syrup, melted coconut oil or vegetable oil, applesauce, eggs, and vanilla extract.
Pour the wet ingredients into the dry ingredients. Stir gently until just combined. Be careful not to overmix.
Gently fold in the diced strawberries.
Divide the batter evenly among the muffin cups, filling each about 3/4 full.
Bake in the preheated oven for 18-20 minutes or until a toothpick inserted into the center of a muffin comes out clean.
Remove the muffins from the oven and allow them to cool in the tin for a few minutes. Then transfer them to a wire rack to cool completely.
These Healthy Strawberry Muffins are made with whole wheat flour, oats, and natural sweeteners like honey or maple syrup. They are packed with juicy diced strawberries, which provide natural sweetness and a burst of flavor. These muffins are a great way to incorporate fruit into your child's breakfast. They can be enjoyed fresh out of the oven or stored in an airtight container for a few days. They make a nutritious and delicious breakfast or snack option for kids.

Thank you for choosing to embark on this culinary journey with me and for entrusting me with a small part of your kitchen adventures.

Your support and trust mean the world to me. Every recipe, every technique, and every story shared in this cookbook is a reflection of my passion for food and my desire to bring joy to your tables. Your decision to purchase this cookbook not only encourages me to continue sharing my culinary knowledge but also supports the countless hours of recipe testing, writing, and photography that went into its creation.

Wishing you many happy moments of deliciousness and culinary creativity!

For Zian And Milan, who brings smiles to my face and joy to my heart every day

www.ingramcontent.com/pod-product-compliance
Lightning Source LLC
Chambersburg PA
CBHW081236080526
44587CB00022B/3957